A FALCON FIELD GUIDE™

ELK

Jack Ballard

FALCONGUIDES

GUILFORD, CONNECTICUT
HELENA, MONTANA

AN IMPRINT OF GLOBE PEQUOT PRESS

To buy books in quantity for corporate use
or incentives, call **(800) 962-0973**
or e-mail **premiums@GlobePequot.com.**

Photos by Jack Ballard and Lisa Densmore
Text design: Sheryl P. Kober
Project editor: Julie Marsh
Layout: Sue Murray

Library of Congress Cataloging-in-Publication Data is available on file.

ISBN 978-0-7627-7422-7

Printed in the United States
10 9 8 7 6 5 4 3 2 1

To George D. Ballard Jr., my father, who loved elk

Contents

Chapter 6: Elk and Other Animals

Chapter 7: Elk and Humans

The bugle of a big bull elk is a sound you'll never forget.

Introduction

My earliest memory of a national park involved an elk. On a rare vacation, my family motored to Yellowstone National Park for a long September weekend. As we wound along, frost glittered on flaxen grass in the meadows, and stately, emerald evergreens stood tall and motionless on the hillsides. The sun shone brightly in a cloudless blue sky.

Suddenly, my head nearly banged the front seat when my father slammed on the brakes of our big 1972 Chrysler. With urgency in his voice, he commanded us out of the car. Confused, we bustled out behind him, wondering about the cause of this emergency. "Look," he ordered.

Gazing in the direction of his pointed finger, I beheld the first living bull elk I'd ever seen. Goring the earth in a tiny meadow with its antlers, the bull lifted its head. Tilting its muzzle, the resplendent animal shattered the morning's tranquility with a resounding bugle. Its breath froze as a great, billowing plume in the frosty air. Even as a second-grader, I knew I'd witnessed something spectacular.

Since that first encounter, I've observed elk for more than four decades. I've watched herds of wapiti (the American Indian word for elk) grazing alpine pastures in Colorado's Rocky Mountain National Park and glimpsed them in the dark timber of Olympic National Park in Washington. I've spied elk in both of the Dakotas—in Theodore Roosevelt National Park in the north, Custer State Park in the south—and in countless locations in our national forests.

I'm thrilled every time I see them. This book is offered in hopes it will similarly inspire your own admiration and understanding of these magnificent creatures, no matter where you encounter elk.

CHAPTER 1 Names and Faces

Names and Visual Description

"Elk" is the name given to a large, hoofed animal of North America. Elk are predominantly brown in color, although their bodies exhibit varying hues. The neck and head of an elk are typically dark brown or chocolate colored. The back and flanks vary from a rich, light brown to tan. Males have antlers and often appear lighter than females on the body, with sides sporting a very pale tan variation or a noticeably yellow coloration. The legs and underbelly of elk are dark, corresponding in color to the hair on the neck and head. Elk rumps appear large and pale in comparison with the rest of their body. Thus, mature elk exhibit a three-toned

The coat of a fat and sleek bull elk appears reddish brown in summer.

appearance that lightens when viewed from the front to the rear of the body: dark brown on the head and neck, medium brown to tan on the sides, followed by a lighter, cream-colored or yellowish rump. During the few months of summer that elk are adorned with a shorter hair coat, their overall coloration is more golden or reddish than at other times of the year.

Misapplication of British or European names to North American wildlife was quite common when non-native peoples began to settle this continent. Such was the case with elk. "Elk" is actually the word used by British and European people of the colonial era for moose. Incorrectly applied to the more widely distributed elk, the name stuck. Thus, there are currently two species of large, hoofed mammals in the world called elk. Moose, known by the scientific name *Alces alces,* are called elk in Europe. The elk of North America bear the scientific name *Cervus elaphus* or *Cervus canadensis.*

In assigning a scientific name to North American elk, some biologists prefer *Cervus elaphus,* the same title given to the red deer of Europe, a species that has a noticeably different appearance than North American elk. Proponents of this name note that elk and red deer can interbreed, producing fertile offspring. Scientists championing the *Cervus canadensis* nomenclature point out the obvious physical differences between red deer and elk that would indicate separate species. They further note that while many species of other animals can interbreed and produce fertile offspring (mallard ducks and pintails, for example), the mere fact that two species can interbreed isn't sufficient reason to classify them as a singular species. So much for the scientists agreeing on everything!

To avoid confusion, many European writers use the name "wapiti" to refer to North American elk. Wapiti is perhaps the most common secondary name or nickname for elk, and perhaps the most logical moniker when speaking of the species in an international context. Originating from the native tongues of the Shawnee and Cree Indians, wapiti means "white rump" and refers to this conspicuous portion of an elk's anatomy.

Within the species, male elk are known as "bulls." Females are called "cows," and babies are referred to as "calves." Sounds just like domestic cattle, doesn't it? For the first several months of life, calves are easily distinguished from adults not only by their smaller size, but also by their buff, spotted coats.

Related Species in North America

Elk are the third-largest hoofed animal indigenous to North America. The largest, in terms of weight, is the American bison. The second largest is the moose. Both elk and moose are members of the deer family, which also includes caribou, white-tailed deer, and mule deer as species native to North America.

Although casual observers sometimes mistake other species of the deer family for elk or vice versa, attention to the most basic details of identification will eliminate the errors. Moose are noticeably larger than elk. Even if observers are not familiar with the relative size of the two species, they can still easily tell them apart. Moose exhibit a more uniformly dark brown appearance across the body, which sometimes appears almost black. Adult moose have high, humped shoulders, a feature not seen in elk. The shape of their head is different as well. A moose's head looks large in comparison to its body, tapering to a prominent, bulbous snout. Adult moose also have a sizable flap of loose skin that extends below their muzzle called a "dewlap." The shape of the antlers also differs in elk and moose. Mature bull elk sport antlers that appear as a single beam, interspersed with pointed offshoots known as "tines." The antlers of adult bull moose look more like oversized paddles with tines sprouting from their perimeter. Lucky outdoor observers in the Rocky Mountains, the northern United States, and western Canada might see elk and moose at the same time or close to each other as their ranges overlap in these locations.

Of the other three species with which elk share the deer family in North America, caribou are the closest to elk in size. The ranges of elk and caribou overlap in some portions of western Canada. Caribou are smaller than elk and quite dissimilar in appearance. The neck of a caribou is very light, tan or creamy in appearance in

Although also members of the deer family, elk are easily distinguished from (clockwise from top left) moose, caribou, mule deer, and white-tailed deer.

contrast to the dark brown of an elk. While the tail of an elk is very short, rounded, and a bit fluffy looking, caribou have tails that are a bit longer, narrow to a point, and are white on the underside. Both male and female caribou have antlers; cow elk do not. The shape of an adult male caribou's antlers is different from that of an elk. Viewed from the side, a bull caribou's antlers sweep back then forward in an arc shaped like a semicircle. An elk's antlers appear straighter, bending slightly backwards. Protrusions from the main beam of a caribou's antlers are palmated, with short tines looking a bit like fingers on a hand instead of the singular tines extending from the beam of an elk antler.

The range of mule and/or white-tailed deer coincides with elk most places wapiti are found in North America. However, it's extremely difficult to mistake an elk for either of these species of deer or vice versa. Elk are much larger than deer. Both species of deer are uniformly colored across the body, appearing in hues of tan, reddish-brown, or gray, depending on the species and time of year. Neither has the dark neck and head of an elk or the yellow rump.

Subspecies of Elk

Depending on the sensibilities of the biologist, over twenty different subspecies of elk might be recognized worldwide. Some of these subspecies, in Europe and Asia, would not be immediately recognized as elk by someone acquainted with the North American species. Many of these subspecies are European red deer, which, although capable of interbreeding with elk, show significant variations in size, coat color, vocalizations, and also the general shape and size of the bulls' antlers. It is interesting to note, however, that subspecies an American or Canadian would recognize as elk inhabit other parts of the world, including China, eastern Russia, Mongolia, and Kazakhstan.

Within the United States and Canada, several subspecies of elk are recognized to varying degrees by the scientific community. Rocky Mountain elk are the most common, distributed throughout the Rocky Mountains of the United States and Canada. Males

Colorado's Rocky Mountain National Park is an excellent place to view elk of the Rocky Mountain subspecies.

of this subspecies typically achieve both large body and antler size where nutritious forage is available. Rocky Mountain elk are abundant and readily spotted by visitors in Wyoming's Yellowstone National Park and Rocky Mountain National Park in Colorado. In Canada, Banff National Park is an exceedingly scenic place to consistently view this subspecies.

Tule elk are found only in California. They range in pockets across the central portion of the state known as the Central Valley, preferring grassy areas and marshlands. Tule elk are the smallest subspecies of elk, with a typical body mass roughly one-half as large as the Rocky Mountain elk. Bulls of this subspecies also develop the smallest antlers. Reduced to just thirty-two animals in 1895, these unique elk now number more than 4,000 due to conservation efforts. Point Reyes National Seashore and Carrizo Plain National Monument are two protected areas where visitors often encounter Tule elk.

Roosevelt, or Olympic, elk roam the damp, coastal forests of Washington, Oregon, and California. In 1928 Roosevelt elk were transplanted to the Afognak and Raspberry Islands of Alaska. Roosevelt elk have also been reestablished in portions of British Columbia in Canada. These elk sometimes grow to impressive sizes and are considered by many biologists to be the largest of the North American subspecies. A four-year-old bull Roosevelt elk killed on Afognak Island had an estimated weight of 1,300 pounds, an incredibly large animal considering bull elk don't normally achieve maximum weight for several years after their fourth birthday. The desire to preserve habitat for Roosevelt elk was a significant factor in the creation of Washington's Olympic National Park (originally called Mount Olympus National Monument) in 1909. Olympic National Park is one of the best places in the nation to encounter this subspecies.

The final subspecies of elk commonly recognized in North America is the Manitoban elk, which historically ranged across the midwestern United States and plains provinces of central Canada. Manitoban elk are thought to be somewhat larger in body size than Rocky Mountain elk, but the bulls typically produce slightly smaller antlers. Manitoban elk kept on game farms in Canada have been bred to grow exceptionally large velvet antlers (described later in this chapter) and are also prized for the quantity and quality of their meat. The extent to which Manitoban elk remain a recognizable subspecies is debated, as they were essentially exterminated from their historic range. Most of the elk now roaming areas that were home to this plains-dwelling subspecies, such as Wind Cave National Park and Custer State Park in South Dakota, and Theodore Roosevelt National Park in North Dakota, are actually Rocky Mountain elk transplanted from Yellowstone National Park or other locations.

Two other historic subspecies of elk in North America, one inhabiting the eastern forests and the other roaming across the mountains of the arid Southwest and northern Mexico, are now presumed extinct. Eastern elk and Merriam's elk succumbed to habitat destruction and more acutely, over-hunting.

In terms of subspecies, it's important to remember that, with perhaps the exception of Tule elk, it's extremely difficult for even a trained biologist to distinguish one strain of elk from another. Members of the presumed subspecies freely cross geographical boundaries in many places as well. The Cascade Mountains of Washington and Oregon are thought to separate the Roosevelt and Rocky Mountain subspecies, although elk intermingle and freely cross the crest of this range. The situation is clearly similar on the Canadian plains between wild Manitoban elk (if they're considered as an intact subspecies) and Rocky Mountain elk introduced in numerous areas. Thus, while contemplating the various subspecies may be an enjoyable academic exercise, for practicality, a North American elk is just an elk!

Physical Characteristics

Although they often appear larger, adult elk normally stand from around 4 to 5 feet at the front shoulder, depending on sex, age,

Bull elk normally weigh from 30 percent to 50 percent more than cow elk.

genetic endowment, and habitat quality. Measured from the nose to the rump, an elk is actually longer than it is tall, with adult specimens generally stretching the tape from around 6 to 10 feet. Mature bulls are considerably larger than cows of the same age. Males typically weigh from 600 to 1,100 pounds. Normal adult females range in weight from 450 to 650 pounds.

Tule elk of California are noticeably smaller than those found elsewhere in North America, commonly weighing about 30 percent less than these averages. Elk of Alaska and coastal populations in the western United States and Canada may be somewhat larger. Unlike humans, who maximize potential for healthy weight within the first quarter of their lifespan, bull elk continue to grow much later in adulthood.

Elk begin life as spotted, reddish-colored calves who commonly weigh between 25 and 40 pounds. Birth weight depends upon the age and physical condition of the mother, whether the calf is born singly or as a twin, and genetics. Calves retain their spotted coats for about the first three months of age; they are shed around the onset of their first autumn. Thereafter, they exhibit the same appearance as an adult elk in a smaller package.

Antlers and Antler Development

For humans, from native peoples to modern-day hunters to families simply wondering at the majesty of a band of elk in a national park, perhaps the animals' most impressive characteristic is their antlers. These appendages, formed of solid bone and found only on males, begin to grow in the spring or early summer, depending on a bull's age. Male elk have two bony protrusions on their skulls known as "pedicles." Pedicles are found on the top of the head between the ears and well behind the eyes. Shaped like cups and covered with skin, pedicles are the "roots" from which antlers grow.

Growing antlers are called "velvet antlers" for their fuzzy, velvety appearance. This velvety skin is filled with an extensive system of blood vessels that provide nutrients to the rapidly growing antlers, which can grow over an inch per day. In late summer, shifting hormones cause the blood supply to diminish. The "velvet" then sloughs from the antlers, a process that is often aided by the elk rubbing their antlers on trees and shrubs. The hardened antlers that remain are composed of bone. Naturally colored white, they soon take on various shades of brown. The coloration comes from staining and foreign material on the antler; it occurs when bulls rub their antlers on trees or gore the earth with the antlers in preparation for the mating season.

For most bull elk, their first set of antlers appears as single, rather thin spikes protruding from the head. Sometimes they are forked at the top or have multiple tines. True to appearance, yearling bulls with antlers that do not branch are commonly known as "spikes." Those whose antlers bear a single branch at the end are often called "forkhorns." A bull's first set of antlers is usually a foot or two in length and varies in diameter from the size of a broomstick to the size of the handle of a shovel. The antlers begin to grow around the bull's first birthday (usually in June) or slightly thereafter. A growth period averaging around ninety days is common for bulls one year of age. Contrary to popular belief, the number of points on a bull elk's antlers is not indicative of its age. Some yearling bulls sprout antlers that are little more than oversized pencils. I've seen spike bulls with short, very slender antlers in both Wyoming and Montana.

When the bull elk is a two-year-old, its antlers begin to grow earlier in the year, around late April or early May. The growth period is also longer, extending for around 115 days. Antlers of a two-year-old bull are longer, slightly thicker, and more branched than those of a yearling. From the central beam of the antler, several tines or "points" develop. This set of antlers usually contains from three to five points per side. Compared to antlers of older bulls, the two-year-old's headgear is smaller and may also be more brittle toward the tops, resulting in frequently broken tines when these bulls fight for dominance during the fall mating season. Among hunters and residents of rural areas in the western United States, these bulls are often called "raghorns."

Antlers are composed of bone. Their color is derived from staining from bark, soil, or other materials.

Four-year-old bulls normally develop a classic set of mature elk antlers. These usually carry six tines on each side, with the fourth tine generally attaining the greatest length and overall size. Bulls of this age begin growing their antlers a bit before the two-year-olds. The growth phase also lasts longer, now extending to around 140 days. Less frequently, mature bulls develop antlers containing seven or eight points on each side. Antlers exhibiting abnormal configurations, with random tines sprouting perpendicularly to the normal ones or unusual groupings of tines are called "nontypical" antlers. Some nontypical antlers may have ten or more points on each side.

The size and overall mass of a bull's antlers increase steadily until sometime around its sixth set, which require about 150 days to fully develop. Thereafter, a bull's antlers will increase in size and mass for up to another half-dozen years (if it lives that long), depending on the habitat in which an animal lives, its overall health and body condition, and the amount and quality of forage available to it in a given year. Wild bull elk in their prime may develop antlers that weigh over 40 pounds and are more than 5 feet long. Viewed from the front, the antlers may easily be 5 feet wide. Farmed elk fed a diet for optimizing antler growth can carry antlers weighing up to 60 pounds, as much as the weight of an average third-grade boy!

Bull elk shed their antlers every year before growing a new set from the pedicles. Older bulls with larger antlers shed theirs first, usually in mid- to late winter. Complex hormone interactions regulate the shedding of antlers. The level of testosterone, a male hormone, declines dramatically in the winter. This causes the adhesion of the antlers to the pedicles to decrease until the weight of the antlers pulls them from the bull's head. Once one antler falls from an elk with a large rack, its head is immediately unbalanced. If the bull then shakes its head, the other antler usually falls as well. In most cases, the cast antlers of mature bull elk are found in close proximity to one another. Once, while hiking in the mountains of Wyoming, I discovered one antler from a large bull lying within a couple of feet of another. Evidently the bull had dropped both antlers in essentially the same instant.

Elk shed their antlers each year. Shed antlers are sometimes chewed upon by rodents or even elk seeking calcium.

As testosterone levels begin to rise in the spring, the adhesion of the growing antlers to the pedicles becomes very strong. This bond is so tenacious that hardened antlers will break before being pulled loose from the pedicle, a condition that persists until the antlers are cast the following winter.

It has been estimated that a fully mature bull elk expends as much energy to grow its antlers as a cow does to produce a calf. Antlers are the fastest growing animal tissue known to scientists. Because there are similarities between the rapid growth of antlers and certain types of cancer, antler growth has been studied as part of cancer research. Antlers are also the only known appendage of mammals that can regenerate spontaneously, making antler growth an area of study in stem cell research as well. For biologists, elk antlers are fascinating for far more than their magnificent appearance.

Hooves and Tracking

The size of elk tracks varies substantially depending on the age, sex, and body mass of the individual. Adult animals of average size leave hoof prints that measure approximately 4 to 5 inches long and 3 inches wide. The length of the hind print is somewhat shorter than the front, commonly 1/2 inch, and is slightly narrower, although variation may be difficult to discern by the untrained eye. Tracks of large bulls may exceed the average dimensions by 50 percent or more.

Distinguishing elk tracks from other ungulates is a function of both size and shape. Elk tracks are substantially larger than those of deer, smaller than moose. In comparison to both moose and deer, elk tracks appear more rounded in shape. In light snow, mud, or soft dirt, the dew-claws of moose are plainly visible in their prints, appearing as two indentations behind the hoof print. Except in unusual circumstances (deep snow or very soft mud), the dew-claws of elk do not show on their prints. When elk run, the space between the two "toes" on their hoof prints widens and the distance between the prints increases

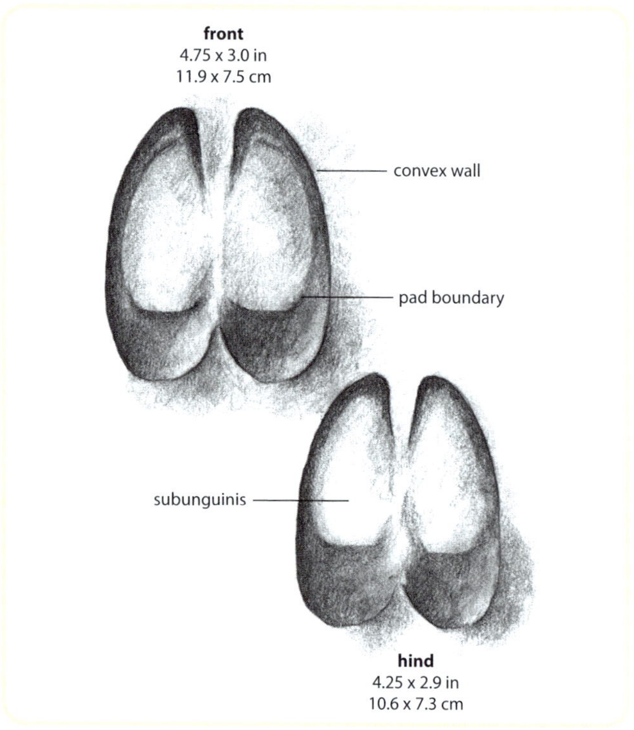

Elk hooves are composed of a hard, outer region with a spongy interior. The two parts of the hoof give elk excellent traction on all types of surfaces from slick, frozen ground to mud.

substantially. To determine which direction an elk is traveling, follow the pointed portion of the hoof print. The hooves of elk narrow toward the front, yielding a simple way to determine their direction of travel.

CHAPTER 2 Range and Habitat

Historic Range

When Europeans arrived in North America, elk were widely distributed across most of the continent. Many modern folks believe that elk are creatures of the mountains. While it's true that in our times mountainous regions of the United States and Canada hold the most elk, these adaptable ungulates were historically at home on the short-grass and tall-grass prairies of the central plains. They also roamed freely across most of the hardwood forests of the East.

In fact it's a little easier to describe where elk were absent prior to settlement. Elk were found in the southern Rocky Mountains of Arizona and New Mexico, with some herds ranging quite far south into mountainous areas of Mexico. However, the animals generally avoided the very arid portions of the desert Southwest. With the exception of small populations in the extreme northern and western reaches of Texas, the largest state in the contiguous United States was devoid of elk.

Similarly, California and Nevada had significant areas uninhabited by elk, namely, the southern and eastern portions of California and much of western Nevada. A band of "elkless" country continued north from eastern California and western Nevada through central Oregon and Washington, a natural "no-elk" zone that likely isolated the Tule and Roosevelt subspecies from the Rocky Mountain subspecies.

In western Canada, elk ranged freely across eastern British Columbia, in all but the extreme northern reaches of Alberta and Saskatchewan, and southeastern Manitoba. Moving east, their historic range uncannily followed what would eventually become the border between the United States and Canada. Elk were frequently found on the south side of the border, but rarely on the north, except in eastern Ontario in the Great Lakes region. The easternmost outposts of historic elk populations ended on the eastern border of New York.

Elk roamed in varying numbers across all of the eastern, southern, and central portions of the United States with the exception of areas adjacent to the coastlines of the Atlantic and Pacific Oceans. They were absent in Florida, but possibly found in low numbers in northern portions of Georgia, Alabama, and Mississippi. Some elk were known to be present in northern Louisiana, which was almost certainly the southernmost extent of their range.

Current Range

With the arrival of Europeans to North America, the world changed for elk. Previously, human predation involved native hunters, skilled in their methods, but not efficiently able to kill large numbers of elk. Settlers not only brought their own firearms, but also put them in the hands of Native American hunters.

Elk are often considered animals of the mountains, but historically, they roamed the plains as well.

The current elk range is expanding in some areas due to natural movement of elk and reintroductions by humans.

Increased taking for food by both native peoples and settlers began to decrease elk populations wherever these large, tasty animals could be killed. By the late 1700s, people were already noticing a decline in elk numbers.

On the plains, huge herds of elk mingled with the seemingly innumerable bands of bison. Both species came increasingly under the guns of subsistence and market hunters in the latter decades of the 1800s. Many elk were killed simply for their two front, canine teeth, which are composed of ivory and were fashionable as adornments to watch fobs.

By 1900 elk were nearly wiped out across most of their historic range. Their strongholds remained in the Rocky Mountains and

Elk from Yellowstone National Park and the National Elk Refuge were used to supplement populations in many areas in the early twentieth century.

coastal ranges in the western United States and Canada, where they were afforded some measure of protection from hunters by terrain less hospitable to humans. The creation of national parks in the mountain states, beginning with Yellowstone in 1872, gave elk a needed buffer from human hunters, although hunting was allowed for a time in some parks. Poaching (illegal hunting) remained a problem for decades. Yellowstone's elk herd and animals from the National Elk Refuge in Jackson Hole, Wyoming, became extremely important for early efforts to restore elk to their native range in other states. In Colorado, for example, elk numbered just a few hundred animals in the entire state in 1910. This remnant population was supplemented with elk from Yellowstone National Park. Nowadays, Colorado has the largest elk population of any state.

Currently, the stronghold of the elk's survival, the Rocky Mountains of the United States and Canada, remains its core area of distribution. Rocky Mountain states and provinces have the largest numbers of elk. Colorado's herd is estimated at almost 300,000 animals, essentially twice as many as any other state. Roughly estimated, states and provinces with between 100,000 and 150,000 elk (ranked from most to least numerous) include Montana, Oregon, Idaho, and Wyoming. New Mexico, Utah, Washington, and British Columbia (again ranked in order of most to least numbers) hold between 50,000 and 80,000 elk. Arizona, Saskatchewan, Nevada, California, and Kentucky are home to between 10,000 and 25,000 elk. Around fifteen other states and provinces have smaller herds of elk. Like those roaming the woodlands of Kentucky, elk in these areas are the products of transplanting efforts.

Fossil records indicate that elk were present in Alaska at the end of the Pleistocene epoch around 10,000 years ago. The dating of one elk fossil in Alaska ages it as 9,300 years old. In 1925 the state of Alaska deliberately transplanted Roosevelt elk to several islands. The most successful of these transplants was on Afognak Island. From a tiny herd of three males and five females in 1929, animals brought from the Olympic Peninsula of Washington, the population burgeoned to over 1,200 animals in 1965, more than the island habitat could support. Since then, the Afognak Island population has fluctuated between similar highs and lows of around 500 animals. Elk have also been successfully introduced to several other islands in southeastern Alaska and have been known to swim between islands.

Elk now roam freely across these Alaskan islands and elsewhere in their historic range due to human efforts to restore them after their distribution was so severely curtailed around the turn of the twentieth century. But elk have done their own part. In many areas in the western United States, elk have naturally expanded their range. When my grandfather homesteaded the ranch of my boyhood west of Three Forks, Montana, just after 1900, elk had been eliminated from this foothills area between two mountain ranges. Crammed into the cab of a pickup with my dad and two brothers, driving up a rough country road on the way to a section of mountain pasture, I watched as my dad slammed on the brakes. Crossing the road in a dusting of snow was a set of elk tracks. It was around 1975. The day after Thanksgiving in 1980, a friend and I spotted four elk, two cows and two calves, on a neighbor's property near the back side of the ranch. Two years later, we saw several cows with spotted calves in the low mountains on and around the ranch. Within a decade, a herd of over a hundred elk roamed the area, much to the delight of my father. With them firmly reestablished in historic habitat, it's now hard to imagine my boyhood neighborhood without elk. Wapiti have similarly moved into new territory of their own accord in many places throughout the western states, a pattern now repeating itself in other locations in the United States and Canada, where they have been recently transplanted into their historic range by wildlife management agencies.

Wildlife observers have plenty of options for seeing elk, some of the most reliable of which are in national and state parks. In the United States and Canada, wapiti are regularly seen in the following national parks and monuments and other public lands: Rocky Mountain and Great Sand Dunes (Colorado); Crater Lake (Oregon); Olympic and Mount Rainier (Washington); Point Reyes, Carrizo Plain, and Redwood (California); Yellowstone and Grand Teton (Wyoming); Glacier (Montana); Theodore Roosevelt (North Dakota); Wind Cave and Custer State Park (South Dakota); Dinosaur (Utah); Grand Canyon—South Rim (Arizona); and Banff and Jasper (Alberta, Canada). Visitors desiring to see elk in eastern national parks should focus their efforts on Great Smoky Mountains (North Carolina) and Buffalo National River (Arkansas).

Elk Habitat

Something to eat, water to drink, a safe place to rest, and room to roam are the basic components of "habitat" for all living things. Various species may have very specific needs in relation to the four basics of food, water, shelter, and space. A ground squirrel, for

Reliable sources of drinking water are an essential element of elk habitat.

example, doesn't need lots of area in which to roam or a standing water source, because it can get its required moisture from the consumption of plants. Elk, by contrast, need reliable water sources and hundreds or thousands of acres over which to range in search of forage. Although they definitely prefer specific things to eat at various locations and times, elk are quite flexible in their diet, one of the factors that, historically, allowed them to colonize most of the contiguous United States.

Habitat types or ecosystems are variously classified by biologists, but certain recognizable areas that contain consistent types of plant life (due to such factors as temperature, annual precipitation, and elevation) are cited as differing types of habitat. In the United States and Canada, forests and prairie (grasslands) comprise the dominant types of habitat. Forests consist of deciduous or coniferous trees or a combination of both. Prairies

Elk are very flexible in their diet, a factor that accounts for their ability to live in many diverse habitats.

vary from regions dominated by shorter grasses to a few remnants of tall-grass prairie in the central United States.

Elk are highly adapted to thrive in virtually every type of forest and prairie habitat, although certain areas, such as high-elevation forests, are inhabited only in the summer months. Foothill regions, often a mixture of deciduous and evergreen trees, along with brush and mixed grasses, are favored by many elk herds as wintering areas. Elk are seldom found there at other seasons of the year. Historically, elk thrived on the grasslands in the breadbasket of North America. However, with the exception of national parks and other reserves, few elk now inhabit the prairies. Areas of intense agricultural production and ongoing human disturbance make it difficult for elk to exist in these places. Like people, elk are happiest when they have the right things to eat and a generous measure of personal space!

REINTRODUCTION

The topics of elk range and habitat touch upon more than simply elk biology. They're also at the core of some of the most controversial issues related to elk. Hunters, wildlife lovers, and certain conservation groups such as the Rocky Mountain Elk Foundation would like to see elk restored over much more of their historic range. However, reintroduction efforts in the central and eastern United States have often met with significant opposition. Wildlife management agencies in some states don't feel they're adequately equipped to deal with lots of critters as large as elk. Few areas in the East offer elk lots of room to roam without encountering farms and highways. Hitting a deer with an automobile is bad enough. Plow your sports sedan into a 700-pound bull elk, and the damage to the car and

Elk have been introduced into the eastern United States, though their presence isn't without a certain amount of controversy. This particular herd roams a private hunt club in New Hampshire.

potential for injury to the driver increase substantially over banging a buck deer.

Crop damage by elk is another significant issue related to expanding elk herds, either through deliberate introduction to an area devoid of wapiti or in areas where elk are increasing their geographic distribution on their own. Elk have voracious appetites and are very fond of

No matter where they live, politics and public opinion affect the health and survival of elk.

many agricultural crops, including alfalfa, oats, corn, and other grains. A few years after elk recolonized my family's western Montana ranch, my dad became a little less fond of the herd of big brown critters that grazed tons of forage from his hayfields. East of Billings, Montana, colonizing elk have taken a liking for cornfields, resulting in extensive damage to the crops. The elk hide in the

fields by day and feed by night. Efforts to haze them from the fields with helicopters or by other means are very expensive. Should farmers be able to kill elk that jeopardize their livelihood?

Elk are also extremely hard on fences. They can jump well but often seem a bit lazy about clearing fences, knocking down rails and ruining the effectiveness of barbwire. I once watched a herd of fifty elk hit a barbwire fence (that I'd recently repaired) at full tilt. The top wire was pulled loose from the posts for nearly 100 yards.

In some places, elk also wreak havoc on landscaping. In Estes Park, Colorado, for example, elk wander through town, chewing up unprotected shrubs and trees, and damaging golf courses.

There are places suitable for elk that are already highly inhabited by people who drive cars and tractors, and who may not want the headaches associated with elk. In these places, it often becomes a matter of politics and public opinion whether wapiti are welcome to the neighborhood.

CHAPTER 3 Forage and Nutritional Requirements

Nutritional Requirements

Elk are large animals with correspondingly large appetites. Various sources estimate the total food intake of an adult elk differently. Some report 15 pounds per day, others as high as 30 pounds per day. However, no single estimate of mass (in pounds or kilos) adequately captures the nutritional requirements of an elk on a single day. The amount of food an elk needs to consume depends on a variety of factors such as its age, its weight, and the quality of forage it's consuming. Total nutritional demands for adult bulls and cows vary considerably over the year. Cows nursing calves

Adult elk can easily consume 20 pounds of forage per day.

require more food than those that are not. During the period of antler development, bulls need greater amounts of high-quality, high-protein forage. Elk on winter range tend to eat about half the amount they consume during the summer months. As a general rule, it's probably safe to conclude elk need about 3 pounds of forage per 100 pounds of body weight per day to remain healthy.

Digestion

Ruminants are a class of animals that digest their food in a two-part process. After consumption, the food is partially broken down in the digestive system, and then regurgitated and

Elk often spend their resting time chewing their cud.

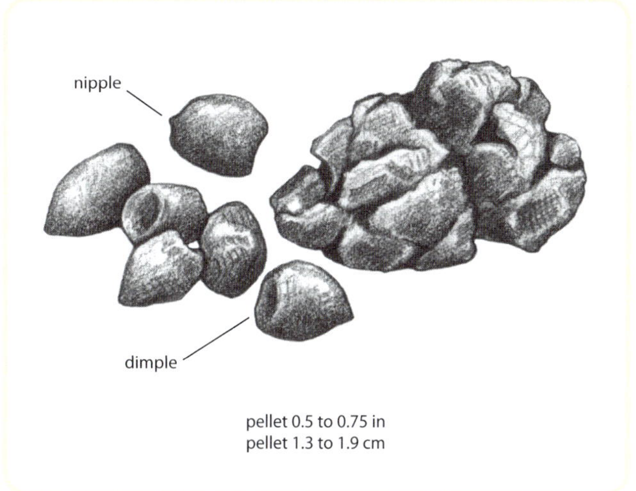

Elk scat may appear in clumps or piles of pellets. If an animal defecates while walking, the pellets may be scattered along a trail several yards long.

chewed slowly to further enhance digestion. It's then swallowed and further digested in a manner similar to that of humans and other nonruminant animals. Elk are ruminants. Watch a herd of resting elk on a grassy hillside in the summer at midday, and you'll probably see many of the animals chewing, though they haven't eaten anything for over an hour. These elk are chewing their "cud," which refers to the partially digested plant matter they regurgitate for further chewing.

An elk's stomach is composed of four compartments, one of which acts essentially as a storage chamber for forage that has been eaten, but not yet rechewed. The other three compartments regulate and complete the digestive process.

Although seemingly inefficient (who needs four stomachs?) the digestive system of elk is remarkably adapted to their diet and daily routines. The expansive digestive chambers allow them to consume large quantities of forage. As much of what elk eat would be difficult to break down into usable nutrients in a simpler digestive system, or might contain potentially toxic chemicals, the slow but tenacious digestive mechanisms of elk allow them to gain nutrition from a wide array of sources.

The product of digestion, elk scat, appears as oval-shaped pellets ½ inch to ¾ inch long with a nub on one end and a dimple on the other. When forage is moist, the pellets may be clumped together.

Food Sources

Ruminant species vary widely in their selection of suitable food sources, a factor that has some bearing on the shape of their muzzle. Bison and domestic cattle are sometimes known as roughage feeders or grazers, which refers to their ability to consume lots of grass and low-growing plants, a habit aided by their large, wide muzzles. On the other extreme are selective feeders or browsers. These animals, like white-tailed deer, are quite selective in the types of plants they eat. They also like to nibble twigs, leaves, and berries from trees and shrubs. Small, narrow muzzles give them the physical ability to be very discerning in the types of plants they consume, and even in the parts of the plants they eat.

Elk fall somewhere in the middle. As intermediate or mixed feeders, elk can graze quite efficiently on grasses and low-growing plants in mountain meadows or on the prairie. They're also very adept at browsing, happily nipping tender shoots and twigs from a wide array of deciduous shrubs. Elk can even strip bark from trees for nutrition, similar to beavers. On many occasions I've observed fallen aspen trees in the fall and winter in elk country. The exposed portions of these trees have been stripped clean of their bark by elk. Elk will also chew bark from living trees, though much less efficiently than from those that have fallen. Lichens and the needles from evergreen trees can also be eaten by elk. Have you ever seen an elk chewing on a bone? Bones and shed antlers are sometimes gnawed upon by elk, a behavior believed by biologists to be motivated by a demand for more calcium in their diet.

A Colorado bull elk chews bark from a fallen aspen branch.

Food sources high in nutrients needed by elk at certain phases of their life cycle or plants generally high in nutrition are favored by elk over less-nutritious forage. Elk certainly can't read nutrition information about the food they're eating, so how do they uncannily choose the best forage? Controlled tests indicate these preferences, at least in relation to unknown plants, aren't based on taste or smell. Rather, biologists believe elk select plants that don't cause gastric discomfort and quickly lead to a sense of satiety or feeling full. Elk have highly developed memories related to the location of excellent forage, sometimes returning to very small areas every year to consume seasonal plants. For three years in a row, I found an identifiable band of bull elk (recognizable by the unique antlers on two of them) grazing on a tiny bench on the side of a mountain in the very early days of July. Evidently there were plants in this tiny area that the bulls loved and they remembered exactly what time of the year they developed.

In the spring elk spend an average of thirteen hours per day foraging.

Forage through the Seasons

The fact that elk can, and do, eat from a wide range of sources gives them great flexibility in their diets, enhancing their survival in habitats less friendly to ruminants with more specific dietary needs. This helpful adaptation is amply illustrated in the ways the eating habits of wapiti change during different seasons of the year.

With the coming of spring, the low-lying areas upon which elk typically spend the winter become tinged with green. The greening of the hills spells early plant growth, usually in relation to early-season grasses. As the soil warms, other grasses and forbs (broad-leafed plants that aren't grasses) begin to grow as well. Elk love these greening plants due to their superior nutrition over the old, bleached grass from the previous summer. They probably also enjoy their tender texture and taste. Toward the end of spring, when all seasonal plants are green and growing, elk become more selective, choosing species such as various clovers and grasses containing very high nutritional value. Spring is a time of intense feeding activity for elk, the animals seeking to regain body mass lost during the rigors of the winter. Elk spend around thirteen hours per day foraging in the spring.

During the summer, elk continue to eat large quantities of grass and forbs, but browse (buds, twigs, and leaves) from deciduous shrubs and trees also becomes an increasingly important part of the diet. Cows with calves demand additional rations of high-quality forage to produce milk for their growing offspring at this time. The nutritional requirements of bulls also change. Extraordinary amounts of protein are required to nourish growing antlers. To adequately support growing antlers, bull elk must consume at least 100 grams (3.5 ounces) of protein every day. However, due to the abundance of food available during the summer and its generally high quality, elk spend considerably less time foraging than they do during the spring. On average, about ten hours of an elk's day in the summer is devoted to eating.

Autumn brings increased feeding activity among elk. The average feeding time per day is nearly thirteen hours. The animals evidently feel the need to maintain the fat reserves they

Elk feed actively in autumn, seeking to gain fat reserves for the coming winter.

gained during the summer or increase them if possible. Elk feed eclectically from grass, forbs, and browse during the fall, orienting themselves toward food sources containing the best nutrition. Some grasses, for example, will sprout new shoots during the fall

ISSUES AND ELK

WINTER FEEDING

In some cases, the number of elk able to live on a region's summer range exceeds the capacity of historic wintering areas. Agriculture, energy development, and human housing have greatly reduced the scope of elk winter range in many places. Although highly winter-resistant under normal conditions, elk can starve to death during extreme winters.

Hunters and wildlife watchers want to see elk. To avoid losses from winter mortality, some states have feeding programs. Hay or food pellets are distributed for wintering wapiti. This allows more animals to survive the winter and increases elk densities on summer range.

However, these feeding programs are not without their critics. For one thing, they introduce a very artificial component that changes the natural fluctuations in elk populations triggered by habitat conditions that may vary from one year to the next. Feeding programs also concentrate many animals in a very small area. Not only does this increase their impact on local vegetation, it also facilitates the spread of disease and parasites. Diseases transmitted through physical contact are much more easily spread between animals when there are large herds of elk in a single area.

Critics of elk feeding programs often point to the bigger problem: lack of suitable winter range. They argue that limiting development on winter range and restoration efforts through habitat improvements such as controlled if there's sufficient moisture and the temperature remains high enough to promote growth. Elk enthusiastically consume these tender, nutritious shoots. In areas of agriculture, elk are highly prone to invade alfalfa or wheat fields that contain green plants.

burning are much better approaches to maximizing the number of elk inhabiting a particular region. One of the largest and most well-known elk feeding grounds is on the National Elk Refuge near Jackson, Wyoming. Although a major attraction for winter visitors and useful in maintaining high elk populations in the surrounding mountains, the feeding of elk in this valley has been increasingly criticized in recent years for its potential to facilitate disease transmission and for its concentrated impact on local habitat.

When snow depths reach more than a foot, pawing through snow makes it difficult for elk to reach forage underneath.

The snowy, cold days of winter represent one of the greatest challenges to an elk's survival. In most places, both the quantity and quality of forage available to wapiti in the winter are at their lowest points of the year. Elk need to conserve energy during the winter. On average, they spend just nine hours per day foraging. While it seems reasonable to conclude that elk should actually

When snow becomes deep or in areas of limited grass, elk readily turn to browse for winter nourishment.

spend more time feeding during the winter to take in calories to stay warm, due to the decreased abundance and lower quality of winter forage, it's really more efficient for them to conserve their resources. Thus, elk pass about thirteen and a half hours of a winter day at rest in a bed, nearly four hours more than at any other season of the year. Elk readily consume grass, deciduous browse, pine needles, and lichens during the winter. To some extent, their winter forage preferences are determined by snowpack. Once snow reaches a depth of around a foot, it becomes easier for elk to browse from shrubs above the snow than paw through it to reach grasses underneath.

Due to local and regional habitat conditions, the forage patterns of some elk may vary significantly from those described above. Elk in northern Idaho, for example, routinely encounter deep snows. Their winter diet thus consists primarily of browse. Elk in prairie habitats have greater access to grass and forbs the entire year than browse. Browse is thus a less important part of their diet than it is for elk in western Oregon, where browse is often more abundant than grass. Eastern populations of elk exhibit similar foraging strategies that exploit the most readily available foods with the best nutrition. Elk transplanted to eastern states devour acorns during the fall, an exceptionally nutritious food source available only in areas containing oak trees and produced sporadically in relation to local growing conditions.

Migration

Many populations of elk inhabiting mountainous areas are migratory, a phenomenon directly related to nutrition. During midsummer, mountain-dwelling elk in the Rocky Mountains are often found at or above timberline. In addition to nutritious alpine grasses and forbs, wapiti favor the high country for its cooler temperatures and lower concentrations of biting flies and other parasitic insects. However, elk are not equipped to deal with 6 to 10 feet of snow that might blanket these summertime haunts in the winter. Thus, they migrate to lower elevations with less snow.

Elk in many mountainous areas use the alpine zone during the summer but migrate to lower elevations for the winter.

However, unlike the more predictable migrations of many birds, elk don't descend to their winter range strictly in relation to the calendar. In fact they'll often stay in the high country long after most people think. Late one October in the Snowcrest Mountains of southwestern Montana, I spotted a herd of thirty elk bedded on a rocky knoll above timberline. To my surprise, a brace of burly mountain goats were bedded around 100 feet below these alpine-loving elk.

What triggers the migration of elk from higher to lower elevations? A highly respected biologist with the Wyoming Game and Fish Department once told me he believes it's a variety of things. The depth of snow cover is perhaps the factor that contributes the most, probably followed by cold temperatures and declining forage availability at higher elevations. Some small bands of elk in Rocky Mountain National Park don't migrate at all; they stay in high-elevation areas where the wind blows the snow from the grass.

In the springtime, a reverse migration occurs as winter snowpack retreats to successively higher elevations. Elk follow the retreating snow (or greening grass) up the mountains. During both seasonal migrations, bull and cow elk behave somewhat differently. Mature bulls remain at slightly higher elevations during the winter, probably due to their longer legs and stronger bodies, which allow them to navigate deeper snow. They also tend to be the first to drift back toward higher elevations in the spring. These seasonal movements from summer to winter habitats occur among many elk populations. Other migrations are more spectacular. Elk in Montana and Wyoming sometimes move over 50 miles between their summer and winter range.

CHAPTER 4 Abilities and Behavior

Physical Abilities

Elk cannot sprint as fast as a pronghorn, nor can they leap as high as a white-tailed deer or mountain lion. Nonetheless, in relation to their size, the physical abilities of these large animals are nothing short of amazing.

Bounding adult elk can cover up to 14 feet in a single stride. Bulls are thought to be a bit swifter of hoof than cows, capable of bursts of speed up to 45 miles per hour. However, evidence suggests that cows and older calves are capable of running longer distances at sustained speeds than bulls. This is certainly true in late summer, when bulls in good habitat have much higher percentages of body fat in relation to cows that have been nursing calves. Elk can maintain speeds of 30 miles per hour for extended periods of time.

Fleet of foot, elk can sustain speeds of 30 miles per hour over long distances.

Although elk are very fleet of foot, their endurance is perhaps more exceptional than their speed. During the settlement of the West, hunters on horseback sometimes pursued elk. Historical records indicate that horsemen riding notably fast, well-conditioned horses could run down elk on the plains, which they sometimes lassoed for sport. However, in terrain broken by hills or in rocky areas, the speed, endurance, and agility of elk were greater than those qualities in the horses. Rarely could mounted hunters catch elk under these conditions.

On several occasions, I've had the good fortune of observing the running abilities of elk firsthand. One time, I frightened a band of several dozen elk in open, mountainous terrain. In a matter of a few minutes, the animals had descended a deep drainage divide, had crossed a sizable creek, and were trotting up a distant drainage nearly 2 miles away. A cousin and myself once watched a herd of cow elk, caught between two parties of hunters in the mountains, scale an incredibly steep chute leading to a knife-edged ridge. Legs churning, rocks and gravel hurtling down the escarpment from their passage, the beleaguered elk finally scaled the ridge and plunged over the other side. Eyeing the chute afterward, it seemed a mountain goat might successfully ascend it, but had we not witnessed the spectacle, neither my cousin nor I would have believed elk could scale the route.

While hiking in the Black Hills of South Dakota, my older brother spotted a band of a dozen cow and calf elk feeding just below the brink of a hill beneath a scattering of large boulders. Suddenly the elk fled in alarm. A mountain lion leapt from the top of the rocks, intent on one of the calves. After just a few leaps, it abandoned the chase. Recounting the incident to me back at our campsite, my sibling reported he was much more impressed with the speed of the fleeing elk than the spectacular leap of the lion.

In addition to their running ability and endurance, elk are very comfortable in the water, easily fording streams and rivers. Their swimming prowess is outstanding. Hypothermia represents an extreme danger to humans in cold water, but body fat and hollow hair not only insulate elk in frigid water but also make them very

Elk are very comfortable in water and are capable swimmers.

buoyant. The spring migration routes of elk often include rivers. At this time of year, streams may be running out of their banks, swollen from snowmelt and very deep. Young calves are frequently confronted with crossing these swift rivers. Just a few days after birth, calves are highly capable swimmers, although young calves often take hours (sometimes days) of encouragement from their mothers before they'll attempt a difficult crossing.

The same notable endurance that allows elk to cover long distances swiftly and efficiently on foot also aids them when swimming large rivers or lakes. Elk on Afognak Island in Alaska have been documented swimming to Kodiak Island, 3 miles away.

In addition to swimming and running, another remarkable physical feature of elk is the strength of a mature bull, particularly in its neck. The neck muscles of a large-antlered bull must support heavy antlers throughout most of the year. (Just think how strong your arms would be if you had to carry 20-pound weights in each hand all day, every day.) During the mating season, or "rut," the circumference of a bull's neck increases dramatically. These overdeveloped neck muscles are used when it thrashes limbs from small evergreen trees and gores the earth so fiercely as to dislodge large clumps of soil. One fall, I watched a very large bull engage its antlers on the underside of a fallen tree trunk appearing some 8 inches in diameter. With a powerful thrust of its neck, the animal launched a section of the partially rotted log into the air. When bull elk fight, one of their primary strategies is to attempt to twist the head of the other animal and throw it to the ground, a task accomplished through the use of their powerful neck muscles. In rare cases, one bull exerts enough force on the other to break its neck.

Vocal Communication

Speech is thought to be one of the abilities that separates humans from the rest of the animal world, but many other species of mammals also communicate verbally. Elk are no exception. A diverse range of grunts, barks, and whistles are all used by elk for various purposes.

The bugle of a bull is an iconic symbol of autumn in elk country.

The mostly widely recognized and dramatic form of elk vocalization is the bugle. Bull elk "bugle" primarily during the mating season to announce their presence to other bulls and the cows a dominant bull gathers together in a group known as a "harem." The bugle of an elk is a drawn-out, rather high-pitched whistle that carries for remarkably long distances. Older bulls often punctuate the end of their bugle with a series of deep, guttural coughs or grunts. In general the bugles of younger bulls are more shrill and lack the resonance of a large bull, although the tonal quality of the bugle is not always indicative of the size of the elk. On a number of occasions, I've witnessed very large bulls with somewhat shrill-sounding bugles. No matter the specific tone, the bugling of a bull is one of the iconic symbols, in sound, of autumn in elk country.

Bull elk also communicate with another sound less easily heard during the rut. Large bulls attending a harem of cows keep the females from abandoning the group and other bulls from intruding upon their cows. To chase a yearling bull (spike) from the cow herd, the dominant bull will rush at the youngster with its lips curled back, nose up, and front teeth exposed in something of a snarl. These visual cues of aggression are accompanied by a distinct hissing sound. Cows that stray from the herd are prodded back toward the group, sometimes quite aggressively by the lord of the harem, who will hiss at unruly cows in the same manner as at small bulls. However, when another bull more close in stature to the herd bull approaches, the keeper of the harem announces its presence and displeasure with bugles and dominance displays rather than hissing noises.

Elk vocalizations aren't reserved just for the bulls. Cows and calves communicate with audible sounds as well. When alarmed, cows emit a very loud call that might best be described as a nasal bark. Depending on its intensity and the setting, the alarm bark creates instant alertness in an elk herd or sends them running in panic.

Cows also communicate with their calves. When separated, cows may call to their calves with a less strident, drawn-out "cow

Cow and calf elk communicate with a variety of vocal and bodily signals.

call" that has been described by Valerius Geist, an acclaimed elk expert, as a "nasal whine." Calves may respond to the cow calls with their own low bleats. When large herds of cows and calves are on the move, frequent communication of this type between cows and calves is quite common and apparently serves as a bonding and reassurance function as well as a locating call. Additionally, distressed or lost calves may emit a very loud bleat while attempting to locate their mothers. However, this communication strategy is not without risk. If predators hear the alarm bleat of a calf, they will respond as quickly as the mother, hoping to find an easy meal.

Since ancient times, exploiting the vocal communications of elk has been a strategy employed by human hunters. Most effectively used during the rut, the hunter may employ either a bugle or a cow call to attract the attention of elk. The bugle is an effective method of locating the general area of a bull. If the hunter imitates a bull's bugle and another bull responds, it is often a simple matter to ascertain the bull's position. Moving closer, the hunter tries to incite a herd bull to come out from its cows to confront this "rival." However, this strategy is not as simple as it seems. Many herd bulls, feeling pressured by a rival, may simply herd up their cows and move to new territory. Elk have an exceptionally keen sense of smell and acute eyesight. The slightest movement by the hunter or the barest whiff of human scent on an errant breeze will send the elk crashing into cover.

Another hunting tactic involves cow calling. Bulls not attached to a harem during the mating season spend most of their hours on the move, wandering about in search of unattached females. Hearing a cow call, a lone bull will often approach the sound, hoping to find a single female or small herd without a herd bull. Again, it takes a very skillful hunter to successfully employ this method of luring an elk within range of a bow and arrow or rifle. However, mimicking the natural noises of elk has been a favored hunting technique for its effectiveness and excitement since ancient times.

Herd Behavior

Elk are commonly known as herd animals. While this is true, it's also an aspect of elk behavior often misunderstood. Except during the mating season, mature bulls and cows live separately with notably few exceptions. Bull calves still nursing their mothers obviously stay with the cows. Yearling bulls and some two-year-old bulls also associate with cow herds during the summer season and throughout the winter. Only rarely are bulls of any kind found among the cows during calving time.

Cows live together in herds numbering a few animals or a few hundred animals, depending on the time of year. The largest herds tend to form in the late fall and winter. However, I've witnessed cow/calf bands of one hundred animals in July. Within these female bands, there exists a hierarchy. Older, dominant cows usually lead the herd. They also claim the best foraging spots and bedding areas. Conflict between cows is signaled by the laying back of the ears, often accompanied by the stomping of a front

Crowded conditions and competition for food may incite aggressive behaviors and communication between elk.

foot. If a rival isn't intimidated by these behaviors, the cow will rear on its hind legs and flail with its front hooves. Alternatively, a cow may expose its front teeth to a rival. This signals the elk is about to bite, another aggressive strategy used to assert dominance. These aggressive measures most often occur between cows in competition for food. The more crowded the elk and scarce the forage resources, the more commonly they occur.

With the exception of the breeding season, bulls also form groups. Sometimes known as "bachelor herds," these bands of mature bulls usually number from three or four animals to a couple of dozen. Huge bands of wintering bulls numbering fifty or more animals have been observed in Rocky Mountain National Park. Similar to the cow herds, bulls hold specific rank within the bachelor group. Rank is established between bulls in important,

Sparring between bull elk establishes dominance without the exertion and risk of a full-blown fight.

but generally peaceful, sparring with their antlers. Sparring usually occurs between bulls with antlers of similar size. The bulls carefully engage their antlers, pushing with their bodies and twisting their necks. These contests let bulls know which animal is the strongest and most likely to win should a full-blown fight erupt, a phenomenon witnessed between rivals during the rut. Like cows, bulls exhibit aggressive or competitive behavior with visual clues, most commonly by quickly bobbing their antlers forward toward an opponent. Bulls may also use exposed teeth as a warning, similar to cows.

Although they don't talk or wave good-bye, elk communicate vocally and with visual cues, just like humans. You'll know you're well on your way to becoming an expert observer of elk when you can predict behavior based on vocal or behavioral cues!

CHAPTER 5 Reproduction and Young

The Mating Season

Although baby elk are born in late spring, the reproductive cycle begins early in the fall. Somewhere around the end of August (varying slightly in relation to latitude, nutrition, and other local conditions), hormonal changes begin to prepare both bulls and cows for breeding. The necks of bulls swell considerably, and by early September, they begin to exhibit aggressive behavior such as raking their antlers on trees, goring the ground and small shrubbery with their antlers, and bugling. Overheated by the physical exertions associated with these activities, they sometimes take mud baths in bogs or wallow in damp areas or small springs to cool off. Within a week or so, they join the cow herds. Large herds of cows may become splintered, as even an extraordinarily large and imposing bull can seldom hold together a harem of more than two dozen cows, although, in some cases, dominant bulls may have harems of over forty females. Less dominant bulls may manage to gather a small band of a half-dozen cows.

The size and number of harems, and the age and strength of bulls required to hold a harem, vary depending on elk numbers in a region, the age and number of bulls in a population, and the ratio of males to females. In areas where the average age of bulls is just a few years old due to hunting pressure, a three-year-old bull might successfully defend a harem. In wilderness areas receiving little hunting pressure or areas where elk are protected from human hunters, such as national and state parks, a bull will have few breeding opportunities until it reaches a more advanced age.

Somewhere around the middle of September, approximately a week or two before the autumnal equinox, bulls enter the period of maximum reproductive behavior, which usually lasts from around twenty to thirty days. The "rut" technically refers to this season of intense reproductive activity. As individual cows within its harem come into estrus, the bull mates with them. Thus, an exceptionally robust bull may sire more than two dozen offspring. Cows that do not conceive a calf in this breeding period may come into estrus around a month later, in mid- to late October. Other cows might enter estrus slightly later than the rut due to lower body condition. Cows carrying low fat reserves will not

Rubbing antlers, goring the ground, and wallowing in mud are all common behaviors of bull elk entering the rut.

With little time to eat and constantly on guard against rivals, a mature bull may lose 200 pounds during the rut.

enter estrus at all. Given all these variables, the entire breeding season for elk in a particular area might span six weeks or more.

The rut is an intensely important part of a bull's life. Those males who compete successfully during the mating season pass their genes to subsequent generations of elk. However, being at the top of the reproductive heap doesn't come without cost. Bulls immersed in the frenzy of the rut spend very few hours per day feeding. Those tending cows expend incredible amounts of energy, not only in the act of reproduction, but also in repelling rival bulls and chasing wandering cows back into the herd, not to mention antler-rubbing, bugling, and other dominance displays. An active, mature male of the wapiti species may lose up to 20 percent of its body weight during a forty-day span in the breeding season. For a very large bull, this might represent a loss of 200 pounds. (Wouldn't fad diet programs for humans love to legitimately claim equally impressive results!)

Reduced body condition and injuries sustained during the infrequent fights occurring between evenly matched bulls during

Exhausted and alone, this large bull broke an antler tine in a fight during the rut, making it difficult for him to compete for a harem.

the rut can literally cost a stag its life. Unless they can regain weight quickly after the rut, a challenge due to poorer forage quality in late fall than during the summer, mature bulls often enter the winter with minimal fat reserves. During a severe winter, many of the bulls at the top of the dominance hierarchy during the rut are at the greatest risk of starvation. Puncture wounds, sprained limbs, or loss of eyesight incurred from the antlers of a rival during a fall fight may prove lethal to the winner due to infection, inability to forage efficiently, or predation later on in the winter.

Pregnancy and Gestation

Cow elk usually become fertile during the fall of their second year in life, the same time that their male counterparts are carrying their first set of antlers. However, unless these yearling cows have had access to quality forage and have attained good body condition, their first successful pregnancy is not likely to happen until the following year. Conception and carrying a calf to birth is also related to body condition in mature cows. Numerous studies of wild elk have shown that conception rates among cows are highly correlated to weight. Undernourished cows have difficulty both becoming pregnant and carrying a calf to birth. During years of poor forage conditions due to drought, cows nursing calves are often among those who fail to conceive next year's offspring. Cows in less than optimal body condition also tend to enter estrus later in the rut, delaying the birth of their calves by a month or more in relation to their healthier counterparts.

Gestation, the length of time between breeding and birth, is usually given as 255 days for elk. At least one study under controlled conditions has placed elk gestation slightly shorter, at around 247 days. For naturalists, an approximate gestation of eight and a half months gives a good estimate of the time between breeding and birth for elk.

Cows in good body condition are more likely to conceive and birth a calf than those who are undernourished.

Nutritional stress during the winter may cause cow elk to birth lightweight, weak calves with a reduced chance of survival.

A cow elk requires a substantial increase in available energy and nutrition to successfully carry a fetus to birth. If the calf is growing inside the cow during the season when it's most difficult to obtain nutrition (winter), how can it hope to meet these needs? At least two important factors facilitate the development of the fetus during this demanding time. Under normal conditions, cows are at their fattest and healthiest going into the winter, giving them energy reserves beyond their daily intake of forage. Also, the fetus develops very slowly for the first 150 days of gestation. At this point, the developing calf only weighs about 5 pounds, or 10 to 15 percent of its birth weight. Beginning around the first of March or the last three months of a cow's pregnancy, the fetus develops much more rapidly. This increased growth normally coincides with rising temperatures and decreasing snow depth on elk winter range, reducing the amount of energy a cow needs to maintain itself and allowing more to be invested in the rapidly growing fetus. However, late winter and early spring nutritional stress on pregnant cows can cause them to abort their fetuses or birth weak, stunted calves with reduced potential for survival.

Birth

The birth of an elk calf is known as "calving." Normally, the first of June represents the pinnacle of calving activity among wild elk. However, some yearly and local variation in this date exists due to the nutritional state of cows during the breeding season and pregnancy, along with other local variables.

Most elk calves weigh from 30 to 35 pounds at birth, though some calves occasionally nudge the scale beyond 40 pounds. Weights vary in relation to numerous factors. Female calves weigh slightly less than males. More significantly, older, larger cows tend to produce larger calves than their younger, smaller counterparts. Good nutrition during pregnancy increases birth weight, but only to a small degree. Twins are relatively uncommon among elk, especially in relation to other members of the deer family, such as moose, mule, and white-tailed deer. Biologists estimate that fewer than 1 percent of the calves born to elk are twins. Calves dropped by cows in poor condition may sometimes weigh as little as 15 pounds. Malnourished calves have little chance of survival. Research indicates that when birth weight drops below 25 pounds, calves have less than a 50 percent chance of survival, even in the absence of predators.

In many populations, nearly two in three births occur in a span of three weeks on the fore and aft sides of Memorial Day. Biologists refer to such a profusion of young born in a short period as "synchronous breeding." Research reported by the Wildlife Management Institute from a number of studies indicates that whether it's a herd in Canada's Banff National Park, the dense woodlands of northern Idaho, Montana's famed Madison River valley, North Dakota's Theodore Roosevelt National Park, or the lofty mountain vales of northwestern Wyoming, the majority of elk calves birthed in a given year fall to the earth moist and wriggling from late May to early June. Elk calves born later in the summer are more apt to starve their first winter than those born around the first of June. Later-born calves don't have as much time to grow and develop as those born earlier and enter the winter smaller and weaker.

STAY AWAY!

The beginning and end of the reproductive cycle of elk are especially interesting to humans. The drama of bugling bulls, occasional fights, and increased visibility of these magnificent animals during the rut draw many people to elk country. In national parks and other protected areas, elk become very tolerant of humans. However, it's terribly unwise to approach a bull elk during the rut, no matter how docile it seems at the moment. Some bulls are very aggressive toward humans by nature; others can become so with seemingly little provocation. In both Yellowstone and Rocky Mountain National Parks, I've observed bull elk chase interloping humans. I once witnessed a bull elk ramming a vehicle with its antlers. Bulls are usually satisfied with simply running a terrified human from their vicinity, but actual goring can occur. For your own safety, relish the spectacle of the rut from a distance. If a bull acts aggressively, retreat quickly and immediately. If you do, the bull believes your threat to its harem has passed and it will normally retreat to its cows.

Newborn and very young elk calves are cute. Spotting them is a treat for wildlife lovers, some of whom may be tempted to approach the calves for photos or better observation. Leave them alone! Causing a calf to move increases the possibility of its being sighted by predators. What's more, cow elk can become aggressive when their calves are threatened. Elk do not differentiate between the approach of a harmless human and a hunting wolf. Both experiences are very stressful for both cows and calves. Even cows that appear to be alone in late spring should be avoided as they may have a calf hidden nearby. For their sake and your safety, stay away.

A few weeks after birth, young calves rejoin the cow herds.

Cow elk typically return to known "calving grounds" year after year. A few days before calving, female elk leave the cow herd. Calves are born in solitude, usually within a few hours of the onset of labor. Extremely vulnerable immediately after birth, the fate of the calf is often tied to the experience of the mother. Cows birthing their first calf or those enduring a difficult pregnancy may abandon the calf altogether, or fail to give it adequate maternal care during the first critical hours of life.

At birth, calves are nearly scentless. Their spotted coats blend with the sagebrush or tall grasses in which they're commonly born. Elk calves can stand within twenty minutes of birth, but for the first several days of life, they spend most of their time hiding from predators. Remaining motionless for most of the day, a newborn calf spends limited time with its mother. The pair is together only for several brief periods of nursing lasting just a few minutes at a time. Within a week, elk calves can run fast enough to elude most predators. About this time, the cow and its new calf rejoin the cow herd from which it departed to give birth.

For the first two months of life, the elk calf's growth is highly dependent on its mother's milk. The volume of milk available to the calf is greatly determined by the quality of forage the cow has to eat. In subsequent months, the calf becomes increasingly able and willing to forage on its own. By the end of its first summer, an elk calf's juvenile spots disappear. Although elk calves are nutritionally independent of their mothers by this time, they generally remain in a herd with their mothers through their first winter.

CHAPTER 6 Elk and Other Animals

Elk and Other Ungulates

Wherever they live, elk share their world with other hoofed mammals (ungulates). Some of these, such as bison, are much larger than elk. Others, such as antelope, are relatively small. Elk compete with some ungulates for food; with others they merely share habitat at certain times of year and have little or no discernible relationship. Along with wild species, elk also share their range with domestic ungulates in many places, primarily cattle and sheep.

In relation to other wild ungulates, the interaction between elk and mule deer is probably the topic of greatest concern to biologists and wildlife managers. Over the past few decades, elk populations have risen dramatically in many places, coinciding with a decline in mule deer numbers, leading some to conclude that large numbers of elk have a detrimental affect on mule deer.

Overlap in diet between the two species certainly exists and may suggest competition for the same forage, in which case it is assumed that the larger elk would have an advantage over deer. Under typical conditions, mule deer consume more browse from shrubs than elk. However, it's important to remember that elk are very adaptable animals in terms of diet and will readily consume a wide range of foods. In locations where browse is the primary source of nutrition on winter range, some biologists believe elk compete directly with mule deer for forage and ultimately displace them.

Although generalizations about rising elk numbers negatively affecting mule deer are misguided, in certain locations there seems to be a legitimate concern. Research conducted on the Mount Haggin Wildlife Management Area in Montana demonstrated a significant amount of overlap between the two species with winter forage. Antelope bitterbrush, the shrub representing the highest percentage of mule deer diet during

Competition from elk browsing on shrubbery is thought to negatively impact mule deer populations in some areas.

the winter, also composed the greatest percentage of elk forage. In mild winters, there's usually enough food to go around. But this study, and some others, indicates that in difficult winters, an abundance of elk may negatively affect the survival odds of mule deer.

Competition between elk and other ungulates, such as white-tailed deer, antelope, caribou, or moose, for food or space is unlikely. Occasionally, elk may face off with bison in meadows for pasture or passage. The diets of elk and bison overlap significantly, although with the exception of Yellowstone National Park and a handful of other refuges, bison do not exist in enough numbers to affect elk. When rare confrontations between elk and bison occur in these places, large bull elk are sometimes able to intimidate female and young bison. In most cases, elk give bison wide berth.

Similar diet overlap occurs between bighorn sheep and elk, both of which species consume large amounts of grasses.

Direct competition on winter or summer range for forage would certainly favor elk, although little study has been undertaken concerning this potential relationship.

On both public and private land, elk frequently utilize the same range as cattle. For the most part, elk and cattle don't mix. Both casual observation and research support this notion. One section of mountain pasture on my family's ranch is grazed by both elk and cattle. When the cows are rotated to this area for grazing, the elk tend to move elsewhere. Elk often exhibit signs of anxiety or heightened alertness in the presence of cattle. Some biologists argue this behavior is more a function of cattle's proximity to people and the trappings of human civilization than the domestic cattle themselves. In certain areas, elk have developed a stronger tolerance for cattle than in others. However, it's unlikely you'll routinely observe elk in the same proximity to

In Yellowstone National Park and a few other places, elk share habitat with bison. Conflicts between the two species are rare.

cattle as that which they comfortably maintain with other wild ungulates such as deer and moose.

Parasites and Diseases

Like other creatures, wild and domestic, elk are susceptible to numerous diseases and are occasionally plagued by parasites. The number and frequency of diseases among elk have doubtlessly increased since the time prior to European settlement of the United States and Canada. Growing contact between elk and domestic animals and reduction of their historic range have exposed elk to maladies not encountered by their forebears.

Among these diseases, brucellosis is perhaps the most widely recognized and exposes elk to the greatest controversy. Brucellosis is an infectious, very contagious disease that occurs

Brucellosis is a disease that frequently causes cow elk to abort their calves during pregnancy and may reduce elk reproduction in local areas.

in various forms depending on the infected species. In cattle and elk, brucellosis may cause infected females to abort their unborn calves. When infected, slightly more than 50 percent of cow elk will abort their first calf after contracting the disease. Crowding of elk on winter range is a major factor in the transmission of brucellosis among elk. The disease occurs among free-ranging elk only in Yellowstone and Grand Teton National Parks and surrounding areas. Brucellosis was almost certainly first transmitted to wild elk in the area by cattle around the turn of the twentieth century. Maintaining brucellosis-free cattle herds is of extreme importance to ranching in the Rocky Mountain states. The potential of elk infecting cattle with brucellosis may create political tensions in local areas where ranching and wildlife interests collide. Another disease of great concern to domestic cattle operations is bovine tuberculosis. This disease can, and has, infected elk but is quite rare.

Chronic wasting disease (also known as CWD) was first detected in elk at a research facility in Colorado. The disease plagues captive as well as wild elk. Assumed to be caused by an infectious protein, or prion, CWD invades the central nervous system. Extreme weight loss and chronic, heavy salivation are common systems of chronic wasting disease. Since its discovery in Colorado, CWD has cropped up in wild and domestic herds in many other states as well. The exact mechanisms of transmission of CWD from one animal to another are not clearly understood. What is certain is the outcome. Chronic wasting disease is always fatal in infected animals.

Early speculation surrounding the disease raised concerns that it might be transmissible to humans or that it might wipe out entire elk populations. Neither alarm has been warranted. The best medical evidence indicates humans who have physical contact with elk or eat their meat are not at risk of contracting the disease. However, state wildlife agencies often encourage hunters to handle elk carcasses in such a way as to minimize possible exposure to the disease—namely, by avoiding contact with tissue from the central nervous system of animals with CWD.

CWD testing programs for animals killed by hunters are available in most states.

Along with diseases, elk are subject to numerous parasites. A variety of worms, mites, ticks, and other not-so-nice-to-contemplate creatures attach to elk as their hosts. Infections by parasites are sometimes fatal, but in most cases, elk have developed a natural resistance to the parasitic creatures in their historic habitat. However, parasites and the transmission of CWD are perennial concerns with elk reintroductions from one area to another. After a small herd of elk was transported from Wyoming to Michigan in 1918, for example, biologists observing the animals in later decades noticed severely ailing animals exhibiting signs of meningeal worms. This parasite commonly occurs among white-tailed deer in the eastern half of the United States, animals generally unaffected by the parasite. Elk moved from one location to another are potential carriers of exotic parasites to the new location or may be exposed to parasites to which they are unaccustomed.

Elk and Predators

A variety of predators prey upon elk. In North America these include coyotes, wolves, mountain lions, black bears, and grizzly bears. Healthy newborn elk have much more to fear from fellow creatures than foul weather. In one research study in north-central Idaho, approximately 70 percent of the calves marked by researchers were killed by predators, mainly black bears. Although predation rates are normally lower than this, in certain areas predators claim a substantial percentage of the calf crop. Interestingly, well over half of the calf mortality occurred in the first ten days of life. Within just a couple of weeks of birth, elk calves develop the speed and endurance to elude all but the most tricky or tenacious attacks from their predators.

Given elk vulnerability in the days just after birth, biologists theorize that the synchronous breeding of elk ensures that some significant percentage of the calf crop will reach the age that makes them less susceptible to predation. Birthing numerous vulnerable prey in a short period of time makes it more likely that some of them will escape detection by predators until they're mature enough to successfully flee. To borrow an analogy from an Easter egg hunt, consider two different strategies. In one, five children have just twenty minutes to find 200 eggs hidden in a backyard. Across the street, egg hunting is a weekend-long affair. On Saturday and Sunday, twenty-five eggs are hidden four times each day. The five youngsters can search for the eggs as long as they like. In which case will the greater number of eggs be found? Conditions being equal, the children with more time to discover what amounts to the same number of eggs scattered over a longer period of time will be more successful. Similarly, synchronous breeding stacks predator evasion in favor of a larger number of elk calves, even though there are actually more vulnerable young

Grizzly bears are major predators of elk in some areas, preying heavily upon newborn calves in the first few days of life.

ISSUES AND ELK

WOLF PREDATION

For the past two decades, wolves have been increasingly multiplying throughout the Rocky Mountains, due in part to natural colonization from Canada via northwestern Montana, and also to deliberate introductions in Yellowstone National Park and wilderness areas in Idaho. The growth of wolf populations has been phenomenal. However, in some regions wildlife managers feel there are too many wolves. Abundant wolf populations have been linked to severe elk declines in Montana, Idaho, and Wyoming where elk are also hunted.

How many elk are enough? What share should go to wolves versus other predators, including humans? These are highly contentious issues. To one extreme are pro-wolf groups who feel wolves should never (or rarely) be killed by humans. To the other extreme are anti-wolf individuals, including some hunters and livestock owners, who feel wolves should be completely eliminated wherever possible. Currently, many other elk predators such as black bears, mountain lions, and coyotes are subject to hunting, one means of balancing their impact on elk numbers against competing human interests.

In many rural communities across the West, elk meat, the product of human hunting, is an important source of highly nutritious, low-fat protein for many families. Outfitting companies also have a vested economic interest in maintaining high elk numbers. In some places,

on the ground at peak calving time than there would be if the birthing period was prolonged.

Although their role is hotly debated in public circles, the increasing number of predators in recent decades has placed wolf predation has significantly reduced the number of elk available to human hunters. Many hunting families would like to see more elk and fewer wolves. On the flip side are people who believe wolf predation ultimately makes elk herds healthier by culling weaker animals and will actually benefit wapiti in the long run. Increasingly, wildlife management agencies are caught in the middle of competing interests when it comes to wolves and elk. Surely there's a biologically sound solution somewhere in the middle that balances wolf and elk numbers. Given the emotions competing sides have around the issue, the "happy medium" is difficult to find.

Wolves prey effectively on elk, especially in the winter when they target young animals and those that are weak.

pressures on reproducing elk not seen since settlers and market hunters overran their habitat, eliminating wolves, mountain lions, and grizzly bears in the process. As more natural populations of these predators have increased due to widespread legal protection, it has become more difficult for elk calves in many areas to survive until their first birthday.

When wolves were introduced into the Yellowstone ecosystem in 1995, biologists had the opportunity to study the impacts they were having on elk populations. Initial research showed that the wolves routinely preyed on older and weaker animals, reducing the number of elk in the northern Yellowstone herd to levels more in line with management targets. Wolf advocates pointed

Elk calves, especially those of small size, are more easily taken by mountain lions and other predators than healthy adult animals.

Large herds of fleeing elk create confusion for predators, making it difficult for them to target a single animal.

out that grizzly bears, not wolves, were wreaking the most havoc on newborn elk.

While that conclusion is supported by a number of studies, it fails to note the impact of wolves on calves in their first winter. Cow/calf ratios among elk are an extremely important indication of a herd's viability. When the ratios fall below levels in the 20 to 30 calves per 100 cow range, most elk herds begin to decline in numbers, even if the hunting of antlerless animals by humans is severely restricted. Thus, surviving the first wave of vulnerability to predation in the first weeks of life isn't necessarily the most important hurdle calves must clear to reach the age of reproduction. Calves must also dodge predators throughout the rest of their first summer and winter.

Once winter hits, wolves become the dominant predator on elk calves, with coyotes also capable of picking off these smaller, weaker animals, which are less able to flee through deep or crusted snow than their adult counterparts. Several studies have found wolves prey heavily upon elk calves during their first winter. In fact wolves show their strongest selection, or preference, for elk calves versus adults when available. Winter wolf predation, in many areas, is a very important factor in limiting the percentage of calves that survive their first year. In addition to bears, wolves, and coyotes, mountain lions also target young elk. Where mountain lions are present in high numbers, they often exert a significant impact on elk survival in their first year of life.

Whether young or old, elk employ a number of strategies to elude predators. Faced with a single wolf, black bear, coyote, or mountain lion intending to kill a calf, a cow elk or group of cows may confront the predator with flailing front hooves capable of delivering a lethal blow to the would-be killer. Bull elk may also fend off single predators with their antlers. However, the best antipredation method employed by elk is flight. Few predators have the speed or stamina to run down a healthy elk, although wolf packs are highly capable of downing adult elk in good condition.

The herding instinct of elk also serves as a buffer against predation. In open country, elk often form large herds, especially in the winter. Many pairs of eyes and ears give them a better chance of detecting advancing predators. Once fleeing, dozens of elk in a moving herd make it harder for predators to target a single animal. The herd also tends to favor the strong and healthy in predator attacks. Old, young, or weakened animals typically fall behind the others when running, making them more easily taken by predators.

CHAPTER 7 Elk and Humans

Elk and American Indians

Interactions between elk and humans in North America extend back into history for a period of some 10,000 years. Artifacts from an archaeological site in Alaska, dated approximately 8,000 to 11,000 years ago, were accompanied by bone fragments from a number of animals including elk. A site in eastern Wyoming from the Folsom era revealed artifacts dated at 10,300 to 10,800 years ago. The Folsom people utilized a unique type of stone arrow point with a groove on either side. A portion of elk antler consisting of a tine from a large bull was recovered from this site. Archeologists believe the antler was used with a simple levering device to create grooves in arrow points.

For the next several millennia, ancient peoples of the North American continent continued to utilize elk for food and parts of the elk, most notably the antlers, for a variety of primitive tools. Elk antlers were used for digging instruments and as tips for fishing spears along with hammering devices. Shoulder blades were fashioned into primitive hoes for cultivation. Although the ability of these primal hunters to kill elk was probably limited, antlers picked up just after shedding were as strong and useful as those taken from a bull killed by arrows or other methods.

The record of interaction between elk and native peoples during the last 500 years is more complete than that of more ancient peoples. From 1500 to 1850, numerous American Indian tribes east of the Mississippi are known to have hunted elk. These include the Sauk, Cree, Chippewa, Huron, Winnebago, Iroquois, and a host of others. Elk meat was a welcome addition to the ordinary diet of these eastern Indians, although wapiti represented a secondary source of food. Elk were difficult for the native peoples to kill. Snares, arrows, spears, and deadfalls (traps consisting of an elevated log that would fall upon an animal when it dislodged a supporting triggering device) are presumed to be methods used to kill elk. The animals were also hunted in the winter when Indians on snowshoes could efficiently overtake elk floundering in deep snow. Some evidence suggests the Indians also obtained elk by surrounding herds and driving them into strategically placed natural enclosures fortified with other materials.

Prehistoric peoples in North America used elk antlers to make a variety of tools.

Prior to being displaced by European settlers, elk were commonly found on the plains, where they were hunted by American Indians.

In the mountainous and coastal regions of the western United States, Indian tribes also hunted elk. In addition to the methods commonly used by the eastern peoples, certain western tribes developed other methods of securing elk. Lewis and Clark observed Indians of the Pacific coastal regions effectively securing elk using pits. Large holes were dug on trails, then carefully disguised with leaves and branches. Elk using the trails would fall into the pits. Some tribes planted sharpened sticks into the bottom of the pit to aid in securing their quarry.

The acquisition of horses by native peoples on the Great Plains dramatically changed their lifestyle. Occurring in the 1600s, this development gave the Indians greater mobility and also a more efficient means of killing large animals, namely bison. However, some of the plains-dwelling tribes, including the Comanche, Kiowa, Crow, and Cheyenne, also used their fleet horses to pursue elk on the prairie.

In various regions, American Indians developed other skillful and opportunistic methods for harvesting elk. Some tribes learned to chase elk herds toward rivers with thin ice, killing the animals that broke through and were trapped. Others deliberately surrounded and pushed elk into lakes and other large bodies of water where they could be more easily killed than in the forest. Some evidence indicates that Indians may have also used "jumps" to secure elk as they did with bison. Jumps were areas where highly orchestrated, communal drives ran animals over cliffs, where they were killed or sufficiently injured in the fall to be easily dispatched. Requiring much effort, well-executed jumps could secure large quantities of food for an entire band of Indians in a single day.

Along with the importance of elk as a food source, Indians prized the animals for numerous other reasons. As mentioned earlier, elk antlers and bones were used as tools. Antlers were also

Elk were prized by American Indians as much for their hides to make leather as for their meat.

The canine teeth or "ivories" were used by many American Indian tribes to decorate dresses.

fashioned into clubs as instruments of war. The saddles of some Indians utilized portions of elk antlers for their framework. Antlers and bones became chisels, wedges, and cooking utensils. Some tribes in California even shaped small, elaborately decorated purses from hollowed elk antlers, which were used to store dentalium shells from mollusks that served as currency.

However, the hides were perhaps the most valuable commodity Indians took from the elk. Wapiti skins were especially prized for their durability. Thicker than the skins of smaller game animals, yet less bulky than the hide of a bison, elk hides were "tanned" by Indians to create exceptionally durable leather. Elk garments, such as jackets for men and dresses for women, were commonly worn in winter due to their weight. The leather from elk also made excellent, long-lasting moccasins. For most tribes, elk garments were not used for everyday wear but reserved for ceremonial purposes and special occasions. Elk skins were used by a few tribes for covering teepees, but this practice was not common and usually applied to the most wealthy and revered members of a tribe.

Wapiti also factored prominently in the social and spiritual life of many Indian tribes. Hidatsa, Nez Perce, Hopi, Pawnee, Crow,

DEVELOPMENT ON WINTER RANGE

One of the greatest survival challenges of elk and impediments to their expansion is winter range. In many regions, elk find plenty to eat in the high mountains during the summer, but much less forage is available at lower elevations in the foothills. Human encroachment on winter range is an increasing problem in many places. Areas with fine mountain views and attractive building sites often sit smack-dab in the middle of elk winter range. Developments for human housing have gobbled up tens of thousands of acres of historic wintering areas across the West in recent decades. Along with housing, energy development on winter range also poses a serious threat to the welfare of many elk populations. Elk that are hunted are naturally shy of humans and their civilization. Human activity around housing developments and energy extraction efforts on wintering grounds scare elk away from needed foraging areas and disrupt migrations. In a few places, such as Estes Park, Colorado, elk habituated to humans winter in suburban areas. However, such cases are rare exceptions. If these magnificent animals are to maintain their current health, citizens and government agencies will need to carefully consider their actions in relation to elk habitat. For most folks, it seems the more intimately acquainted they are with wapiti, the more willing they are to limit personal and economic interests to preserve these majestic creatures.

Flathead, and a host of other tribes had elk societies or religious cults that variously revered and spiritualized the power of the elk. The canine teeth or "ivories" of elk were used as adornments in clothing and jewelry by many tribes. One of these practices involved the sewing of dresses adorned with elk ivories. Worn by women and sometimes children, these garments attested to the hunting prowess of a woman's husband or a child's father and were very valuable. Prior to the late 1800s, men apparently viewed elk tooth adornments as appropriate only for women. However, after the 1870s, men from a number of tribes began to adopt elk tooth jewelry, perhaps in relation to the increasing scarcity of the animals and their ivories. Elk tooth dresses are still fashioned by many tribes today, although the "ivories" are usually artificial.

Elk and European Settlers

Armed with muskets and rifles, European settlers had a much easier time killing elk than did native peoples. In fact the firearms of white explorers and homesteaders were too efficient. Elk were killed for food, but widespread slaughter of elk on the plains for their hides and the two ivory canine teeth hastened the demise of these animals from most of their native habitat.

Many biologists feel that had it not been for the rugged mountains of northwest Wyoming and similar areas in other states, elk might have been hunted to extinction. Protections afforded to the animals by the creation of Yellowstone National Park in 1872 were critical to their survival. Visitors to the park reported a scarcity of game animals in the first decade after Yellowstone's creation. By 1891, however, Yellowstone's gamekeeper reported that elk numbers had increased to an estimated 25,000 animals. In the early 1900s, elk from Yellowstone were relocated to create or augment elk herds in many locations throughout the Rocky Mountains. In Montana, nearly 1,000 elk from Yellowstone were distributed to various regions across the state in 1910. The future of Montana's elk became brighter in 1913 when hunting laws and closures were enacted to protect the animals, a situation that occurred across many western states at about the same time.

The rugged habitat of the northern Rocky Mountains may have saved elk from extinction in North America.

Elk and Us

With the development of hunting laws, concerted efforts to reestablish elk into many parts of their historic range, and greater concern for the preservation of habitat, wapiti numbers and distribution in the United States and Canada have increased steadily for the last century. Currently elk are commonplace throughout the Rocky Mountains and many other places, their health and habitat largely protected by the vigilance of wildlife and land managers at both the state and federal levels.

While estimates of the exact impact vary, elk probably have the greatest economic value for humans in relation to hunting, although elk viewing also brings substantial revenue to many national parks and adjacent communities. Numbers fluctuate

Elk are of extreme economic importance to local communities and state wildlife agencies in the West due to expenditures by hunters for licenses and other services.

annually, but nearly one million hunters take to the forests and prairies of the United States and Canada to hunt elk each fall. Interestingly, there's almost a 1 to 1 ratio between hunters and elk. For every elk in North America, there's one human hunter. As a rough estimate, hunters kill about 150,000 elk per year in the United States and Canada. Some hunters pursue elk strictly for their meat and may expend less than $100 for their hunt, including the cost of the permit, gas, and ammunition for their rifle. Others are highly motivated to obtain an impressive set of elk antlers to display in their home. These individuals, sometimes called "trophy hunters," may spend over $5,000 in search of a trophy bull. Employing guides and outfitters, trophy hunting is an important part of the local economy in many small towns across the western United States and Canada. In addition to hunting, the prospect of viewing wapiti lures tourists and wildlife lovers to various national parks and other reserves across the country, giving elk economic importance beyond hunting.

Index

About the Author

Jack Ballard, author and photographer, has written hundreds of magazine articles about elk, appearing in diverse titles such as *Women in the Outdoors, Wyoming Wildlife, Colorado Outdoors, Camping Life,* and *Petersen's Hunting.* He writes a wildlife column for *Camping Life* magazine and natural history blogs for www.audubonguides.com.

Ballard's photos have been published in numerous books, calendars, and magazines. He has received multiple awards for his writing and photography from the Outdoor Writers Association of America and other professional organizations.

He holds two master's degrees and is an accomplished public speaker, entertaining students, conference attendees, and recreation/conservation groups with his compelling narratives. When not wandering the backcountry, he hangs his hat in Red Lodge, Montana. To see more of his work visit www.jackballard.com.